Finding V :
The Great
Alphabet Hunt

Paula Curtis Taylorson

illustrated by Anna Semenova

Finding V : The Great Alphabet Hunt

This is a work of fiction.

Printed in the United States of America

A 2 Z Press LLC

PO Box 582

Deleon Springs, FL 32130

bestlittleonlinebookstore.com

sizemore3630@aol.com

440-241-3126

ISBN: 978-1-954191-23-5

Dedication

Thank you to those who read to me and those who listened to me read.

This book belongs to:

_____

Vlad is a **vital** market stall **vendor**.
He sells and is **vivacious** while he sings!

He rides around on his **Vespa** scooter,

Collecting **V** words and **various** things.

His sidekick, **Vincenzo**, a **vole** from **Verona** (in Italy), wears a **visor** and a bright hi-**vis vest**.

He's a **valued** and **versatile** employee.
Though his **vision** is poor, he's the best!

In a **voluminous** and busy **village** square,
Vivaldi plays his Stradivarius **violin**.

He plays close to his open
valise and a **variety** of
vacationers drop coins right in!

An old army **veteran**
who is no **vagabond**,
wears his **victory** medal with pride.

He buys some **vivid** and
oddly shaped **vegetables**, and
a **vintage vial** with **vanilla** inside.

A **venomous viper** is charmed out of his basket.

He dances **vertically** to the tune of a flute.

While a **Vietnamese** pot-bellied pig passing by,

videos it all for a Hollywood shoot!

A **vocal vampire** in red **velvet** britches,
visits **Vlad's** market stall in the town.

He wants to surprise his sister **Vicky**
with a **vase** that's **vermillion** and brown.

Vincenzo jumps into his **vibrant vehicle,** a **van,**

and **vanishes** down the **valley** at high speed!

He's **volunteered** to fetch Vlad
varied goods they can sell -

such as **vinegar,
vermicelli,** and flaxseed.

Outside the **Victorian villa** in the square,
blooms a garden with sweet **violets** and **vines**,

and a stall that sells bouquets, **verses,** and **veils,**
is a perfect **venue** for sweet **Valentines!**

The **view** from the **veranda** is **virtual** and clear,
with a **volcano** that is impressive and **vast**.

And a statue of **Venus**, who is armless and **vain**,
stands on the **verge** of a **voyage** to the past!

Then, along came some **vegans,** looking for nuts.

We passed a **ventriloquist** with a doll on his knee,

a **vixen** with three cute fox cubs in tow,

and sat with a **vulture** eating **vindaloo** curry for tea!

All the stalls are now empty, the **Vs** have been sold.

Vitamins, varnish, and vacuums galore!

Search **vigilantly** for the items that begin with a V

and you'll discover

that there's always quite a few more!

The End

My Very Own 'V' Words:

_____

_____

_____

_____

_____

_____

_____

_____

_____

_____

Glossary

Page 1. **Vlad** : a boy or man's name
Vital : one who is important, necessary
Vendor : someone who sells items
Vivacious : lively, active, energetic

Page 2. **Vespa** scooter : an Italian scooter

Page 3. **V** : a letter
Various : different types of items

Page 4. **Vincenzo** : a boy or man's name
Vole : a mouse-like rodent with
short limbs and a short tail
Verona : a city in Italy
Visor : a hat with a brim
Hi Vis vest : a workman's safety
vest

Page 5. **Valued** : what something
is worth or has merit or importance
Versatile : flexible, able to change easily
Vision : able to see with the eyes or
able to predict an outcome of events

Page 6. **Voluminous** : large, open area
Village : a small town
Vivaldi : a person famous for creating music, composer
Violin : a musical instrument, a stringed instrument

Page 7. **Valise** : a small piece of luggage carried in hand
Variety : different types of things to choose from
Vacationers : a time without work to just have fun

Page 8. **Veteran** : someone who served in the military
Vagabond : a poor person, bum
Victory : to win

Page 9. **Vivid** : very clear, easy to see or understand
Vegetables : food
Vintage : something older
Vial : a small plastic container
Vanilla : a flowering plant that an extract is taken from to flavour food

Page 10. **Venomous** : poisonous
Viper : a snake

Page 11. **Vertically** : up and down direction

Page 12. **Vietnamese** : from the country of Vietnam

Page 13. **Videos** : pictures that are like a movie

Page 14. **Vocal** : to make noise, usually sounds
Vampire : a bad person or thing that sucks blood
Velvet : something with a soft feel to it,
Visit : to go and stay with for a short time

Page 15. **Vicky** : a girl or woman's name
Vase : a vessel of ceramic or wood with a wide mouth used to hold flowers or for decoration
Vermillion : a bright red color

Page 16. **Vibrant** : colorful, outstanding
Vehicle : a driving machine, a car, tractor, or other to get to another place in
Van : a large automobile

Page 17. **Vanishes**: disappear, cannot be seen
Valley : a low area of land or water

Page 18. **Volunteered** : to work for free
Varied : many different types of something

Page 19. **Vinegar** : a sour acidic liquid
Vermicelli : pasta, food

Page 20. **Victorian** : a period of art and time
Villa : a small residence
Violets : small purple flowers
Vines : the long slender part of a plant that climbs
and creeps and spreads around a support

Page 21. **Verses** : paper with poetry on it
Veils : light scarfs used to cover the head or face
Venue : a way to find something, a path
Valentines : presents for Valentine's Day Feb 14th

Page 22. **View** : the area that can be seen
Veranda : a porch or terrace attached to a home
Virtual : something real
Volcano : a mountain or hill with a hole in
the top that spirts out lava
Vast : very large area or amount

Page 23. **Venus** : first name of a Greek goddess
Vain : very proud of oneself
Verge : on the edge or rim, or about to
do something, the beginning of something
Voyage : a trip on the ocean

Page 24. **Vegans** : to eat only vegetables

Page 25. **Ventriloquist** : the art of speaking without moving your lips

Page 26. **Vixen** : a female fox

Page 27. **Vulture** : a large bird of prey
Vindaloo : a very hot Indian curry made with meat or poultry, flavored with tamarind, vinegar, and garlic

Page 29. **Vitamins** : essential foods and minerals
Varnish : a substance applied to a surface to coat it and protect it and give it a shine
Vacuums : a object that removes dirt

Page 30. **Vigilantly** : very awake and alert
Also on page 30 : **Veal** : food, young beef
Volleyball : a ball used to play volleyball with
Violin : a musical instrument
Vehicle (bicycle) : a 2 wheeled vehicle to ride

Paula Curtis Taylorson Lives in Marston Mortaine England. She is a full-time secondary school teacher of English and English Literature. She was amongst the first of the initial students to graduate from the Uk's first BA (Hons) Creative Writing Program at the University of Bedfordshire.

Her first love is poetry and rhyme and she works hard to inspire and teach appreciation of the subject to all age groups. Many of her students have gone on to be successful writers.

A2Z Press LLC

A2Z Press LLC
published this work.
A2Z Press LLC is a
publishing company
created by Terrie Sizemore
for the purpose
of publishing literary works by new
and aspiring writers. All content is
G-rated. We welcome your submissions
of ideas for children's literature as well
as adult and self-help topics.
Science and medicine, holidays and
other interesting topics are all welcome.
Submit queries to sizemore3630@aol.com or
PO Box 582
Deleon Springs, FL 32130

www.ingramcontent.com/pod-product-compliance
Lightning Source LLC
Chambersburg PA
CBHW041523120626
46551CB00018B/2549